THE MEANINGS OF MODERN ART

by JOHN RUSSELL

Art Critic, *The New York Times*

VOLUME 11

THE GREAT DIVIDE 1950–70

THE MUSEUM OF MODERN ART, NEW YORK

I. Robert Rauschenberg
Charlene, 1954
Stedelijk Museum, Amsterdam

Copyright © 1975 by The Museum of Modern Art   All rights reserved   Library of Congress Catalog Card Number 72-76416
Series ISBN 0-87070-477-X   Volume 11 ISBN 0-87070-488-5   Designed by Earl Tidwell
Cover: plate V. Jasper Johns, *Flag*, 1954. The Museum of Modern Art, New York

The art of the second half of this century treads everywhere on tender ground. For what is true of people and of public events is also true of works of art: we have a special feeling toward the ones we grew up with.

This feeling is rooted in reason, for it is in first youth that we establish the modes of feeling, the canons of beauty, and the standards of truth and integrity by which we are to live for the rest of our lives. But it also goes beyond reason. We are committed, every one of us, in ways that are sometimes welcome, sometimes repugnant, to what is done in our own day. Its face is our face, its ways are our ways, its echo is the twin of our own. We may demur—"It has nothing to do with me," we may say, whether from modesty or from disgust—but posterity will not believe us. Posterity will say that to be alive at a given time and not to be marked by the events of the day is a disgrace and a diminution. We were there; this and that happened; how could we not bear the marks forever?

This is true above all of those moments in history at which a shift of sensibility occurs or the potential of human capacities is redrafted. People who come to maturity at such times are by that much the more alive. It would, for instance, be a very dull American who did not feel that the first years of the presidency of Harry S. Truman were a time unlike any other. In terms of political, economic and military power the United States dominated the rest of the world as never before or since. It had a primacy of the sort which can turn to tyranny; but the use made of it was more often than not both farsighted and responsible. It was also magnanimous: how often in history has a nation offered to renounce a decisive military superiority in the interests of the common good? Yet this is what happened in 1946. Had the Baruch plan been accepted by the United Nations, the United States would have destroyed her stock of atomic weapons and manufactured no more of them, in return for a general agreement that atomic power should be used for peaceful purposes only, with regular worldwide inspection to confirm that this was being done.

United States policy was magnanimous in other ways also. We should not forget that twelve million American men and women were given the chance of further education under the G.I. Bill of Rights; that relief to the devastated countries of Europe ran at around $700,000,000 a year; and that when George C. Marshall was Secretary of State, in 1947, he made it possible for those same countries to establish, by their own exertions but with American financial backing, "the political and social conditions in which free institutions can exist." That such institutions should exist was much to the advantage of the United States: to that extent the Marshall Plan can be interpreted in terms of American self-inter-

est. But anyone who traveled in Europe in 1946 will know that the condition of victors and vanquished alike was appalling; and to both of them at that time the large-heartedness of the United States seemed as genuine as it was prompt.

It could be a coincidence, but I don't think it was, that American Action Painting came to the fore at precisely that time. Action Painting was not, as some people supposed, melodramatic or self-indulgent. It arose from an intelligent examination, on the part of people who had been serious artists for nearly half a lifetime, as to just why so much of European painting had run itself into the ground. And it stood for an idea current in public life also: that human nature had not said its last word.

Many of its manifestations had an evangelical character. In a major Jackson Pollock, as in a slashing, man-sized, black-on-white Franz Kline, painting comes into the open, baring its essential nature with a mimetic vivacity that can still carry us away. When Arshile Gorky unbandaged the wounds with which life had left him, he did it in such a way that we found new courage to face our own hurts. It was a time for the undefeated spirit. What was called an "American sublime" was brought into being: a mode of expression from which the contingent and the equivocal were banished. A painting like Barnett Newman's *Day One* (fig. 2) is typical of that moment in history. Already its title suggests the beginning of a new era for all humanity; and it was typical of its time in being, as Thomas B. Hess points out, "not only unsaleable, but unexhibitable. There was no chance at all, with its 11-foot height, that it could be sold or even seen by anybody but the artist and the friends he invited to his studio."

The all-or-nothing, backs-against-the-wall character of work such as this answered to experience of life not only during the Depression and during World War II, but even in the late 1940s, when the audience for radically new art in a country of 140,000,000 people was estimated at around 50: "a small circle," as Clement Greenberg described it in the fall of 1947, "of fanatics, art-fixated misfits who are as isolated in the U.S. as if they were living in Paleolithic Europe." Greenberg went on to describe their isolation as "inconceivable, crushing, unbroken, damning"; and it is natural that those who lived through that period either as participants or as sympathizers should consider that later generations of American artists have had a much easier ride. Certainly they have not had to draw for so long on the reserves of moral energy which were demanded of Pollock, de Kooning, Gorky and Newman. Nor were they called upon to make the kind of breakthrough to public acknowledgment which has to be made once and once only; by 1956, the year of Pollock's death, that job had been done. Thereafter it was taken for granted that painting and

3

1. Franz Kline
Painting Number 2, 1954
The Museum of Modern Art, New York

sculpture had a new rank among American modes of expression, and that they were redefining America as distinctly as it had been redefined by Emerson in the 1830s, by Herman Melville in the 1850s, and by Whitman in the laconic penetrations of his *Specimen Days in America* (first published in 1882–83).

It was a lot to ask of any artist that he should do this; but in their different ways—and no group of men could have been more different, one from the other—the American Action Painters had trained hard and long for it. Nor were they in any doubt of the historic and definitive shift in sensibility which they were to bring about: "But surely our quarrel is with Michelangelo!" was Newman's rejoinder when fellow artists tried to scale down their ambitions to a more parochial level.

Theirs was, in fact, a prodigious commitment: but one that was in line with the changes that were coming about in many other departments of life in the late 1940s. "To every age, its own art" had been the motto of the Vienna Secession when it was founded in 1897; and the new American painting lived up to it. If life was different, art would be different too; and how different, how startlingly and unfathomably different was the life that came up over the horizon after World War II! It was not simply that the conditions of everyday existence were changed beyond recognition by antibiotics, by computerization, by the transistor, by the jet engine, by the prospect of atomic power. It was that the ingredients of metaphor had been turned upside down and would never be right way up again. It is by metaphor, and by analogy, that we feel our way through life; yet here were medicines that did away with many of the traditional terrors of illness, machines that performed feats of assimilation previously within the reach of one man in a million, and instruments of the size of a pocketwatch that could do the work of a freight locomotive. Ancient certainties toppled day after day. Standards accepted since long before the name of "American" was first spoken no longer made sense. The power of speedy and nimble adjustment to all this was

4

as much a part of the postwar era as horns are part of a ram. And yet people could become too open to new ideas, too quick to assume that nothing could faze them; and they could end up feeling, with the bemused hero of Saul Bellow's novel *Herzog,* that "modern character is inconstant, divided, vacillating, lacking the stone-like certitude of ancient man, also deprived of the firm ideas of the 17th century, clear, hard theorems. . . ."

A NEW SET OF CERTAINTIES

It was one of the strengths of American Action Painting in the late 1940s and early '50s that it offered, in contradistinction to all this, a new set of certainties: modes of feeling so wide in their range and so peremptory in their expression as to form the apparatus of survival in a world where preexisting landmarks were few. In pictures like Pollock's *Convergence (Number 10, 1952)* and Newman's *Vir Heroicus Sublimis* (Volume 10) feeling was all of a piece, without reserve or equivocation. The new American painting covered the whole gamut of human experience, from the most exalted (Mark Rothko said that "subject matter is crucial, and only that subject matter is crucial which is tragic and timeless") to the undignified and the hilarious. (As much as anyone in modern times—poets, novelists, playwrights not excepted—Arshile Gorky makes clear the often grotesquely inconvenient nature of our deepest entanglements; and it is Willem de Kooning who has best carried forward into our own day the notion, so prevalent in the late 19th century, of the man-eating Venus.)

I have to say at this point that the history of the New York School is neither as simple nor as orderly nor as unified as I have made it appear. Making art is by its very nature an untidy, spasmodic, unequal business; and when there occurs a collective impulse to let more of life into art than had been admitted before, then human frailty is bound to come in along with other and more constructive qualities. The artists of the New York School had their flaws, like the rest of us. Operating on terrain that was largely untested, they found some of it spongy and had to withdraw. They had dry periods, as well as fertile ones. The moral energy which informed their finest works came and went. To speak of them as "a school" is, as I said earlier, a matter more of convenience than of historical truth. Yet one thing was common to all of them, and common to most thinking people in the late 1940s: a feeling of "either/or." In art, as in so many other departments of life, humanity was being given a fresh start. It was time to stand up and be counted; the question at issue was (or seemed to be) *either* a decisive shift in sensibility *or* a genteel continuance.

2. Barnett Newman
Day One, 1951–52
Whitney Museum
of American Art,
New York

5

3. Joaquín Torres-García
New York Street Scene, 1920
The Hirshhorn Museum and Sculpture Garden, Smithsonian Institution,
  Washington, D.C.

The South American painter Joaquín Torres-García was 40 years ahead of Pop art in his appreciation of the New York street scene, with its billboards, its aggressive use of the word writ as large as possible, its insistent numbers and its delight in the flat competitive image.

That was how it looked around the time that Harry S. Truman put the pollsters to shame and got himself reelected by a large majority. By the time that Truman was out of the White House, in 1952, the world looked different. The unified salvationist outlook had given way to misgiving and disquiet at every level of society. The New World fancies of the late 1940s began to look too fanciful by half. Nothing was what it had seemed to be when Marshall was Secretary of State, when the United Nations was an immaculate phantom not yet localized by the East River, and when Southeast Asia was just a place where the French and the British were always getting into trouble. Of course there were still the spectacular novelties of technology: in fact there were more of them every day. But what if they got into the wrong hands for the wrong purposes? What was once called "a full life" was within the reach of more and more people. But what if that life turned out to be not so much full as empty? What if there were some-

thing sterile and self-defeating about the response to life which could be summed up as "I consume, therefore I am"?

In one way and another just about everybody felt let down in the early 1950s, and their feelings were acted out at the level of obsession in the long series of defections and betrayals, real or imagined, which were a feature of the period. Nobody who read, day by day, of the trial of Alger Hiss in the United States and of Otto John in Germany will forget how violent were the passions which these cases aroused. Nor could any scientist be quite unmoved by the fact that Fuchs and Pontecorvo, both men of great consequence in their field, felt it better to leave the West and settle in the U.S.S.R. Something was dying at that time; and that something was the notion of humanity for which Barnett Newman had spoken up in his *Vir Heroicus Sublimis* as recently as 1950–51.

Just what came out of all this in art could be charted, day by day. But in our shorter space it may be more illuminating to follow the example set by Shakespeare's Hamlet when he wanted to explain the difference between his murdered father and his stepfather. Hamlet could talk his way through just about anything, but in that moment of crisis he fell back on the painted image. "Look here," he said, "upon this picture, and on this." It is difficult, admittedly, for us to particularize as exactly as Hamlet did. No one picture will serve for one extreme, no one picture for the other. But we can get some idea of the cross-generational confrontation if we put a late Pollock, *White Light,* 1954 (fig. 4), side by side with *Charlene,* 1954 (pl. I), by Robert Rauschenberg. And it will become clearer still if we go on to put Jasper Johns's *Target with Four Faces* (fig. 6) side by side with Clyfford Still's *1960-R* (fig. 5).

The impact of confrontations such as these has still not subsided. For the older generation, something holy had been defiled. The art historian Leo Steinberg remembers, for instance, "the reaction to Jasper Johns of two well-known New York abstract painters. One of them said 'If this is painting, I might as well give up.' And the other said, resignedly, 'Well, I am still involved with the dream.' He too felt that an age-old dream of what painting had been, or could be, had been wantonly sacrificed—perhaps by a young man too brash or irreverent to have dreamed yet." As for Robert Rauschenberg, he is to this day a non-person to champions of a certain direction in abstract painting: someone not to be named, let alone discussed. These are religious matters, in which loyalties are absolute. "He who is not with me is against me"; and the idea that it is possible to see very great merits on both sides once drew from Harold Rosenberg the rejoinder that "the eclectic critic is guaranteed extinction." On this matter, as

II. Helen Frankenthaler
Other Generations, 1957
Collection the artist, New York

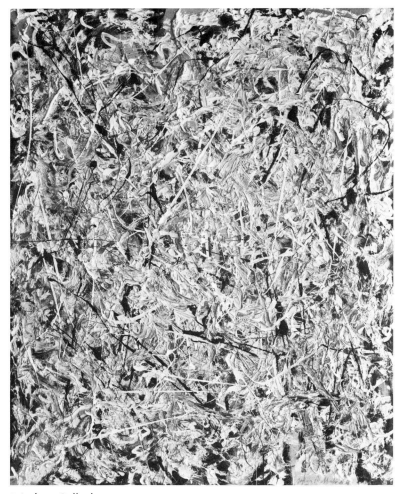

4. Jackson Pollock
White Light, 1954
The Museum of Modern Art, New York

on most others, Rosenberg was categorical: "1946 to 1952 or 1953 was a remarkable period in American art, and no period since has come close to equaling it."

This was in part, as I said earlier, a generational matter. An acute French observer of life, Jean de La Bruyère, wrote three hundred years ago, "We only love once. The other times are less involuntary"; and his remark has not gone out of date. Intelligent people know, of course, that art never stays the same; and they also knew by 1955 that it was time for the logic of history to intervene and bring forward something that had evolved naturally from Action Painting (or from Abstract Expressionism, as it was also called). It seemed most likely that that evolution would start from the basic premise of Action Painting: that the image was generated by the very act of applying the paint, without conscious reference to anything in the world outside the studio and with no concessions to the divide which once separated painting from drawing, foreground from background, and light from shadow. A development of that sort had begun in 1953, in that the concept of staining the canvas, instead of applying the paint to its surface, had been investigated by a painter in her middle 20s, Helen Frankenthaler. Two gifted painters from Washington, D.C., by name Morris Louis and Kenneth Noland, had been to see her work in New York; and it was reasonable to look to all three of them for an uncompromising lyricism that would maintain the level of aspiration which had sustained Rothko and Newman and the others. All this was bound up not only with a specific notion of art but with a specific notion of human dignity; people felt deeply about it then, and they still feel deeply about it now.

But there were other young people—born around 1930, let us say—who had convictions which were no less strong, and no less firmly rooted in their historical situation. As they saw it, Action Painting had sprung from a climate of feeling that was distinctly that of an earlier generation. What had been right for 1947 was not right for 1955, any more than in Paris what had been right for 1905 (the Fauvist exploitation of heightened color) had been right for 1910, when the first masterpieces of Cubism were virtually colorless by the standards of five years earlier. Action Painting had had many facets, but it arose above all from a grand, high-souled opening out of the self which found expression in a large-scale unified eloquence. There were incidental exceptions: in one of his "Women" de Kooning had cut a pair of red lips out of an advertisement and collaged them to the canvas, and if we look closely at the vortex of Pollock's imagery we may find that fragmented objects from everyday life have been sucked into the whirlpool and left there. But fundamentally the materials of Action Painting were those of traditional painting, just as its aspirations were toward the amplest and most spectacular unveiling of an individual human nature.

Great works of art came out of this conviction. But by the mid-1950s it had lost its solitudinous and evangelical status and become an orthodoxy. Just about everyone was trying to act upon it. The "either/or" syndrome had impressed itself on hundreds of more or less gifted, more or less genuine artists, much as Cubism had ceased by 1914 to be an activity for just two or three supremely gifted people. But what if the "either/or" syndrome was not the only answer? When John Cage published *Jasper Johns: Stories and Ideas* in 1964 he put the dissenting point of view in two short sentences: "The situation must be Yes-and-No not either-or. *Avoid a polar situation.*" (The words italicized are Johns's own.)

YES-AND-NO: NOT EITHER-OR

In general conversation these would not be fighting remarks, but in the context of the art of the mid-1950s they caused a cultural divide to crack wide open, sundering father from son, husband from wife, and friend from friend. Too many people had too much at stake for the concept of "yes-and-no" to be accepted lightly. It was on the basis of "either/or" that a whole generation had seen its contemporaries win through to worldwide acceptance. "Either/or" was associated with a virile, fearless, all-enduring turn of mind; what could the "yes-and-no" approach of John Cage and Jasper Johns stand for, if not a flabby, easy-going acceptance? A relaxation of all standards? A readiness to see the barriers go down between art and entertainment, art and interior decoration, art and merchandising? Such things should be resisted; meanwhile there was only one place for art to go to, and only one way for art to get to it.

It was in those terms, more or less, that the alarm was sounded. And there was undeniably a look of provocation about the paintings of Jasper Johns and Robert Rauschenberg when they first went on view. After the American sublime, a facsimile of the Stars and Stripes! After the exalted investigations of Rothko and Still, a bed smeared with paint and hung on the wall! After Gorky had probed the most tender places of the psyche, a target with plaster casts of a nose and a mouth stuck on top of it! Anyone who learned of such things by hearsay might well think of them as acts of sabotage against the high art which had lately won through to recognition.

They were nothing of the kind. There was nothing destructive or nihilistic about Johns and Rauschenberg, and the idea that they could be likened to the Dadaists was wide of the mark. The logic of history was on their side, as much as it had been on the side of Pollock and de Kooning; but it was a logic born of a different view of history. Their work was predicated on the belief that a mixed mode of utterance was true to life as it was being lived, and that it was not the role of the artist to censor and unify a flow of experience which in reality was made up of compound apprehensions which needed to be read in more than one way at once.

This point of view had been touched upon by two pioneers of modern sensibility. It was fundamental to the work of Marcel

5. Clyfford Still
1960–R
The Hirshhorn Museum and Sculpture Garden, Smithsonian Institution, Washington, D.C.

Duchamp that the observer should be challenged to take in several meanings at once, and that these meanings can operate on quite different levels of understanding. (How this worked has been made clear here in relation to *Fresh Widow* and *Apolinère Enameled* (Volume 6). John Cage in the late 1930s had suggested more than once that there should no longer be a point at which life stopped and art began. In 1937, for instance, he foresaw the use of electronic instruments which would "make available for musical purposes any and all sounds that can be heard."

6. Jasper Johns
Target with Four Faces, 1955
The Museum of Modern Art, New York

Musical expression would be set free from the tyranny of existing musical instruments; "we can compose and perform," Cage went on, "a quartet for explosive motor, wind, heartbeat, and landslide."

As between Johns and Rauschenberg, there is no doubt that it was Rauschenberg who took over the Cage position in a wholehearted and singleminded way. In an often-quoted statement he said that he wanted to work "in the gap between art and life"; and in 1961 he told an interviewer that "There is no reason not to

consider the world as one gigantic painting." So far from treating the picture as something set apart from the world, he welcomed the world into it. He saw it as the function of the artist to work with what is given; and in paintings like *Charlene* he sieved the dredged filth of New York City as a prospector sieves the sand of the riverbed: for gold. *Charlene* is as American, and as much a part of the American life of its epoch, as is the page in *Specimen Days* where Whitman describes Manhattan as he knew it in 1879. It is, in fact, a contribution to the roomy, meandering, accumulative tradition of American autobiography.

"Combine-paintings" was Rauschenberg's name for pictures of this sort; and they do, in effect, combine unaltered materials of the most heterogeneous kind with passages of straightforward paintwork. So far from making fun of Action Painting, they are clearly the work of someone for whom the Abstract-Expressionist brush stroke and the look of paint dripped straight from the can are an important part of art: but a part to be taken into the work as a phenomenon among others. It is not for them to bear sole responsibility for the picture; and they are, if anything, all the more eloquent for being made to coexist with newsprint, reproductions of Old Master painting, half-obliterated comic strips and (in *Charlene*) the outstretched spokes of an umbrella which have been fleshed out and painted over and can be spun around like the arms of a windmill.

So dense is the deposit of allusion and association in *Charlene* that we can stay with it for weeks on end and still find new points of entrance, new appeals to memory, new combinations of sight and touch and feel and remembered smell. It is a part of the continuum of big-city experience; and as I said before it treats earlier, pre-existing art as a part of that experience. Art is accorded equality with the rest: no less, and no more. A lost tradition of narrative painting reasserts its rights as we track back and forth in the accumulation of one man's experience. There are elements of abstract painting also in the tall thin vertical panels which structure the painting as a whole; and in the flattened umbrella in the top right-hand corner there is an after-echo of the severe geometrical painting of Europe in the 1930s—a time when *Circle* seemed a predestined name for a good art magazine. *Charlene* is a picture to live in, not to look at; and among the qualities for which it speaks is an open trust in the way things are.

The case of Rauschenberg's *Bed* (pl. III) is comparatively simple, though few works of art have caused so much exasperation. *Bed* is about paint's power to survive, as the instrument of human expression, in surroundings no matter how far removed from those of high art. Action Painting had claimed for the artist, and for what he produces, a place set apart. It relied on materials, and

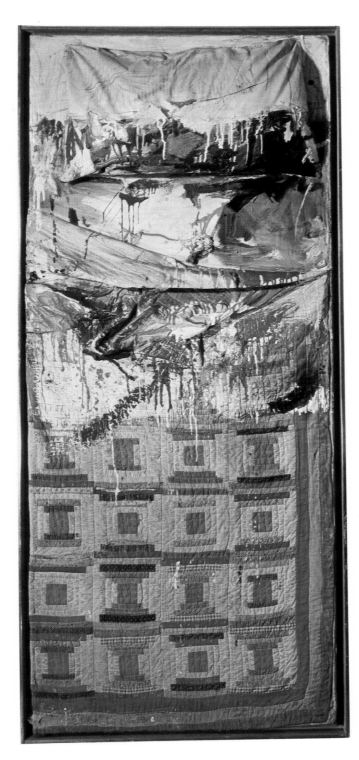

III. Robert Rauschenberg
Bed, 1955
Mr. and Mrs. Leo Castelli, New York

7. Robert Rauschenberg
Empire II, 1961
Philip Johnson, New Canaan, Conn.

Rauschenberg worked for years with Merce Cunningham and his dance company. Cunningham is the agile figure in the top right-hand area in *Trophy I.* And Rauschenberg makes the most of Cunningham's seemingly effortless balance by introducing into the lower left-hand area of the painting an image which is the epitome of ungainliness—a fallen horse and its unseated rider. The point is rammed further home by the sign that reads "Caution: Watch Your Step." In *Empire II* Rauschenberg perpetuates the kind of image which he would improvise from whatever materials came to hand as Merce Cunningham and his company moved from city to city. An object familiar from the New York skyline in its less pretentious days is given a new and altogether grander identity by being mounted on what looks, in this context, to be a rough-and-ready chariot.

8. Robert Rauschenberg
Trophy I (for Merce Cunningham), 1959
Galerie Beyeler, Basel, Switzerland

9. Robert Rauschenberg
Monogram, 1959
Moderna Museet, Stockholm

What is often taken for a classic act of provocation—"The man puts a tire round a stuffed ram and expects us to call it art!"—is in point of fact only one detail in a set of complicated statements. *Monogram* has to be read in several directions at once—as a painting (on the floor), as a collage, as a sculpture, and as a combination of all three. The ram's face is made the pretext for a particularly eloquent piece of pure painting; and as for the alliance of the tire and the ram, it is one of those incongruous conjunctions which had been fundamental to imaginative art for nearly half a century. It shows, also, the unerring sense of drama which Rauschenberg brought to his work in the theater; this is an image that stops the audience talking.

on a specific type of physical construction, that asserted the continuity of high art. Pollock may have spread his canvas on the floor and worked on it in ways that were quite new, but when the picture got up on the wall it was stretched taut and trim on a rectangular wooden support, just like an easel painting by Rubens or Velázquez. *Bed* gets away from all that and asserts, by contrast, that the eloquence of paint can be bestowed on the apparatus of everyday life. The bed in *Bed* is still a bed, but it is also a painting; Rauschenberg here works literally in "the gap between art and life," and he contrives to close it, so that art and life merge into one single experience and can no longer be separated one from the other.

These were difficult ideas, when they were first mooted. Too

10. Robert Rauschenberg
Rebus, 1955
Mr. and Mrs. Victor Ganz, New York

Rauschenberg here takes the detritus of the New York street—a political poster, two news photographs of track events, a comic strip and some objects of more mysterious provenance—and allies them to a small reproduction of Botticelli's *The Birth of Venus* and a page from an art magazine. The great art of the past takes its chance, in other words, with metropolitan graffiti and with the kind of images to which no one gives more than a moment's attention. For all its chaotic appearance the picture is tautly organized and bound together with passages of pure painting.

11. Joseph Stella
Battle of Lights, Coney Island, 1913
Yale University Art Gallery, New Haven, Conn.

much was risked, too much was questioned, too much familiar ground was ruled "off limits." It was not immediately clear to what an extent the epic scale and the exuberant physicality of *Charlene* and the other combine-paintings of Rauschenberg were specifically American qualities that had found a completely new outlet. The facts of American abundance had always tempted American writers, poets, composers and painters, and many of them had tried one variant or another of the cumulative approach: Charles Ives piling one orchestra on top of another, Whitman listing his allegiances for page after page, John Dos Passos apeing the cross-cutting of the cinema in his novel *U.S.A.,* Joseph Stella in 1913 working his heart out to get the whole of Coney Island on canvas (fig. 11). Rauschenberg was in the listing business, too; but he realized, as no one had realized before him, that raw material can be served up raw and that art and life could be made to interlock in the mid-1950s as they had never quite interlocked before.

Rauschenberg at this stage in his career was still very much the boy from out of town who had made it into the big city. He had just discovered the poetics of glut, and he couldn't wait to tell us about them. The paintings were a way of dealing with the unprecedented input that came the way of everyone in the postwar metropolis: and not merely "a way," but the only way of coming to terms with it without censorship or dilution. Rauschenberg gave himself, too: open-handedly. It is the paradox of his combine-paintings that although there is nothing so bizarre or so recalcitrant that it could not find a place in them (a stuffed hen, a deflated inner tube, a radio in full operation) Rauschenberg marks them all with his own identity. He is them, and they are him: the ancient sorceries of art are still in operation.

Rauschenberg's activity is basically outgoing in character. He has a gift for communication and an inbred sense of performance. Extravagances no matter how baroque turned out to end well when he was in charge of them; and when he encroached upon the performing arts—whether as dancer, as artistic adviser to the Merce Cunningham Dance Company, as a founder-member of EAT (Experiments in Art and Technology), and as the inventor of art works that depended in part on activation by their audiences—it was with a consistent optimism.

JASPER JOHNS AND THE READYMADE IMAGE

The case of Jasper Johns is entirely different. He stands for the lapidary, as against the garrulous; for ideas laid one on top of another, as against ideas spread out laterally; and for the thing thought over week after week, as against an overflowing generosity that can survive occasional lapses. Rauschenberg in the mid-1950s was like a faucet of ideas that just couldn't be turned off; Johns was, and is, altogether more deliberate, more self-critical, more apt to say, "Is this really worth doing?"

His work presented from the first the kind of many-layered difficulty which is the surest indication that important art is on the way. The flag, for instance: was it a hoax? An affront to Old Glory? An inscrutable private joke? Discussion waxed hot. In point of fact it was none of those things. It was an intelligent man's response to the fact that the admired painting of the day had to do with images of an entirely idiosyncratic sort: signs never made before. Painting of this kind was running itself breathless by the time of Johns's first New York show in 1958, and in many cases it looked like self-indulgence of Brobdingnagian proportions. It seemed to Johns to be a good idea to see what could be made with an image which was, on the contrary, readymade and immutable. Such an image would ideally have length and breadth but no depth, since the flatness of the canvas was fundamental to painting at that time. If the basic image was so

12. Jasper Johns
White Flag, 1955–58
Mr. and Mrs. Burton Tremaine, Meriden, Conn.

familiar as to bring about a virtual anaesthesia of the aesthetic faculty, people might be confronted as never before with the pure essence of painting: the primal shock for which others had aimed in ways that had begun to look merely rhetorical. The American flag was just right, in this context. It was an image which in itself left almost no one indifferent; yet its associations were so far outside the domains of art as to suspend altogether the traditional art gallery habits of mind. There occurred to every single person, when he first saw one of Johns's flags, a moment of disbelief; and in that moment he was accessible as never before to the primal shock of painting.

As it happened, no two of his flags were the same. People who said "Seen one, seen them all" were put in their places when it turned out that the unchanging face of Old Glory masked a series of raids upon the traditional uses of oil paint, together with a revival of the use of encaustic and a number of forays into territory not yet mapped. There was a ghost-flag—a huge, phantomatic expanse of whites on whites and grays on grays—and there were flags in which faces half-surfaced through the familiar red-and-white horizontals. There were flags on flags, most monumentally superimposed. There were flags which had a private reference, and as late as 1973 there was a double flag which came across with a brilliant, extroverted, public effect. There were flags

which reflected the large areas of melancholy in Johns's own nature; and there were flags which stood for the elemental cachinnations with which in private life, an intermittent melancholy notwithstanding, he seems to reinvent the notion of laughter.

The flags did, however, have one thing in common: they were all painted on a flat, unbroken surface, and they were to that extent traditional pictures with no adjuncts or annexes. This was not the case with the *Target with Four Faces* of 1958, and it was not the case with many other, later works by Johns. The target, like the flag, was ideal subject matter, in that flatness was of its essence. It was readymade and immutable, like the flag; and in its everyday appearances it, too, probed the limits of impersonality. A target which showed individuality would be by that much the less of a target.

A target is made up, on the other hand, of concentric circles, and Johns was far too astute an observer of modern art not to know that concentric circles had been a favorite motif with abstract painters since the days of Robert Delaunay and the youthful Stanton Macdonald-Wright. Concentric circles did away with the necessity for composition, since the form of the image was dictated from the start. They made it possible for each color to "tell" with an intensity that would be modified and weakened if they had to overlap or interlock. In a fine art context they also raised problems which in the past had been solved by giving the circles not the blank, frontal look of a target, but a fragmented or interrupted fine-art look. (This continued to be the case in the late 1950s and early 1960s when Kenneth Noland, for one, was working with concentric circles; he repudiated the unvarying readymade form of the target by varying the internal relationships of one circle to another.) Johns made no claims for this target as art. It was what the title said it was: two pairs of yellow and blue circles, centering on to a red bull's-eye. Their physical substance was mysterious, as was that of the wall-like surface of which they formed a part. There could hardly be a less personal image, and yet the impression which stayed with the observer could be owed to one man only.

Flag and target make demands upon us which have nothing to do with the demands of art, though with the one as with the other we associate an exceptional degree of involvement. When Johns paints them we shift to and fro, involuntarily, between the kind of recognition which is owed to a flag, or to a target, and the kind of recognition which is owed to art. Noticing this, we learn something new about living. In *Target with Four Faces*, Johns thickens this particular plot, and we come to know what John Cage meant when he wrote in his notes on Johns that "I thought he was doing three things (five things he was doing escaped my notice)." For the upper part of this picture is really very peculiar. Where the lower part has the total flatness of a paving-slab, the upper part has real three-dimensional recession: genuine depths in which plaster casts of a sightless head are secreted. This section is hinged, moreover, and has a lid which can be swung down at will. The four heads are identical, and they present themselves to us with an identical frontality. There is the sharpest possible contrast between the shadowed recesses, in which the heads sit in retreat from the world, and the light of open day which floods across the target. The one is a complex scale-model, in full working order, of an inscrutable situation; the other one of the simplest of man-made objects, and one of the most easily explicable. The complete image, as haunting as any in 20th-century art, has overtones of fairground and firing squad, jury-box and old-style pharmacy.

It is basic to the work of Jasper Johns that he makes us question not only what we are looking at but what is entailed in the act of looking. All looking has to do with cognition; but do we look in order to know something completely? Or do we stop looking, in any real sense, as soon as we have made an initial act of recognition? Johns never lets us off that particular hook. Defying us to give in to laziness, he chips away at the sloven in all of us. Take the printed word "Blue," for instance. It is so keyed to our expectations of a certain color that if it happens to be colored red, as may well be the case in a painting by Johns, then we see it as if we had never seen it before.

In the 1960s Jasper Johns began to tackle these questions in bulk and simultaneously, in paintings on the scale of epic which have none of the small-scale concision of his earlier work. But in 1958–59, in his *Numbers in Color* (pl.IV), he was still working with a finite image drawn from the experience of everyday. The series of numerals that runs from 1 to 0 is a sign-language so complete and so nearly universal that it would really be very difficult to get through life without it. Its rival, in this, is the alphabet (and Johns did once make a very beautiful painting called *Gray Alphabet*); but there are several kinds of alphabet, whereas the series 1-0 is as valid for a Russian as for an American, and as valid for a Pakistani as for a Moroccan. It is one of the great instruments of negotiation; without it, we should be stuck with the abacus.

What Johns did in his *Numbers in Color* was to set out the complete sequence from 1 through 0 eleven times over. The subject was *given,* and it recurred with an absolute regularity, just as in a passacaglia the bass line recurs unaltered over and over again. The paradox of *Numbers in Color* is that by accepting this fixed and immutable subject Johns gave himself a freedom of maneuver and an openness of expression which were total and

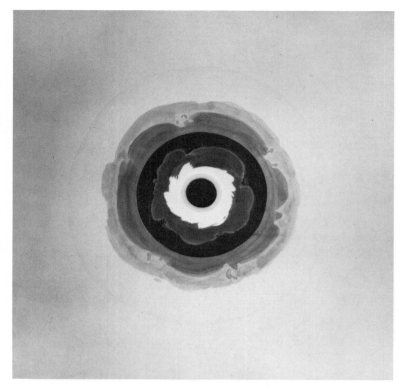

13. Kenneth Noland
Flutter, 1960
Mr. and Mrs. Albrecht Saalfield, Bellhaven, Conn.

When Noland first began to paint concentric circles he allowed (as here) a liberal measure of individuality to his forms, together with a soft, stained after-echo of them which related to Helen Frankenthaler. Soon after (see *Reverberations*; fig. 40) he used an altogether more impersonal mode of attack.

unlimited. We can see just what this means if we compare *Numbers in Color* with Pollock's *White Light*. In the Pollock, freedom of expression is preordained. The painter has no obligations to anything except the dictates of his own psyche. The picture is the paint, and the paint is the picture: nothing else intrudes. And *White Light* is undeniably a beautiful picture, with all the luxuriance which we associate with a major artist who knows exactly what he is doing and is comfortably inside the limits of his potential. It might seem to be enough, and in terms of the embellishment of life it certainly is enough; but art has a higher and a more strenuous function, and a part of that function is to go on ques-

IV. Jasper Johns
Numbers in Color, 1959
Albright-Knox Art Gallery, Buffalo, N.Y.

V. Jasper Johns
Flag, 1954
The Museum of Modern Art, New York

14. Jasper Johns
Figure 5, 1955
Collection the artist, New York

15. Charles Henry Demuth
I Saw the Figure Five in Gold, 1928
The Metropolitan Museum of Art, New York

Demuth's painting of 1928 is on one level a masterpiece of American plain statement and the precursor of much that was done in the 1960s. But it is also an act of cryptic homage to the poet William Carlos Williams, whose name, nickname and initials can all be found in the picture. (Williams had written a poem about how he once saw a scarlet firetruck moving through the city with the figure 5 painted in gold upon it.) Johns's *5* has no hidden meanings and no illustrative intent, but it shows in close-up the attitude to numerals which found such monumental outlet in *Numbers in Color* (pl. IV).

tioning the terms of art's validity. Art survives not because it gives pleasure, but because it goes on asking questions to which we need to know the answer. Pollock in *White Light* was giving pleasure of an exalted, hard-won kind. Johns in *Numbers in Color* gave that same pleasure—the delight of seeing paint handled superlatively well—plus something else. He used the alphabet of numerals to redraft the alphabet of feeling. *Numbers in Color* sets out the gamut of human emotion with reference (and herein lies the contribution of Johns) to an ordered schema from which feeling is traditionally excluded. Emotion plays no part in mathematics. Neither love nor hate will make 2 x 2 equal 5. Numerals are weightless, incorporeal, independent of time and place, above and beyond individual feeling. They form a closed system to which feeling has no access. The impersonal single subject, so valuable to Johns in 1954, was succeeded in 1958–59 by the impersonal system, with its even greater potential.

Questions of identity have always preoccupied Johns, and he is perfectly well aware that each of the ten numerals in question has a personality which is clearly defined. "Number One" stands for leadership, in common parlance, and Johns's number 1 has a broad, upstanding shaft, a sharp downward turn at the top (like the peaked cap of some archetypal field-marshal), and a square-built plinth-type base: all stand up for an impregnable solidity. Zero has also its associations; and Johns drafts a broad-bellied vacancy, an echoing oval that signals a moment of repose after the clattering activity of numbers 1–9. Himself conspicuous in life for sensitivity toward the identity of others, he gave each intervening numeral its own character: we remember, for instance, the enlarged teardrop which forms the stem of his number 7 and the swanlike curve of his number 2. But he tells us explicitly that the picture is about numbers *in color*; and as every word counts in a title by Johns we are warned that the picture is as much about color as it is about numbers.

What Johns does is to animate the entire surface of the canvas with an all-over, in-and-out paint structure which has the vitality of Action Painting but is keyed to something outside itself. There are two separate and independent structures here: on the one hand eleven rows of numerals with their recurrent subliminal crescendo from 1 to 0, on the other the continually varied skeins and loops of paint which sometimes menace, and sometimes give way to, the mathematics of the basic design. Every great painting carries within itself the history of other great paintings; and in *Numbers in Color* we see something of the fugitive and vagabond humors of landscape painting, something of the verticals and horizontals of Mondrian, and something of the patient monitoring which we associate with still life. Everything is there, and every kind of statement. Looking at it, we realize all over again that it is not from the unsupported ego that great art is most likely to come.

There is, of course, an alternative hazard: the artist may fail to impose upon heterogeneous material that imaginative order which is the essence of what we call "art." If too much material is given the right of entry, and if the operating imagination is too weak to deal with it, chaos and triviality will result. The challenge of new and complex subject matter had to be met, even so; the highly energized character of new art in the 1950s made it mandatory. And it was not only Rauschenberg and Johns who gave the signal; on the contrary, the expansiveness, the limitless ambition and the bodily involvement for which Pollock set the defini-

16. Richard Smith
Soft Pack, 1963
The Hirshhorn Museum and Sculpture Garden, Smithsonian Institution, Washington, D.C.

British Pop art is distinguished from its American counterpart by its gentler, more lyrical approach. Richard Smith took the familiar image of a cigarette pack and made of it something which combines the ferocious zig which Noland was to apotheosize in *Plus 10* (fig. 39) with the eloquent staining of an early Frankenthaler (fig. 41). Where American Pop takes a single idea and asserts it as strongly as possible, Richard Smith takes a whole group of ideas and gets them to live together.

17. Louise Nevelson
Sky Cathedral, 1958
The Museum of Modern Art, New York

Louise Nevelson, born in Russia, was five years old when she arrived in Maine as an immigrant. After a spectacularly varied and adventurous career both in this country and in Europe she had her first exhibition of sculpture at the age of 41. The experience of half a lifetime was summed up, therefore, in the tar-black and heavily shadowed walls which she built up, piece by piece, from the debris of junkyard and carpenter's shop. She built them as the tall wooden ships had once been built in the Maine of her childhood; but she added elements of poetical ambiguity which had no place in shipbuilding.

18. Ad Reinhardt
Number 119, 1958 (Black), 1958
The Hirshhorn Museum and Sculpture Garden, Smithsonian Institution,
　Washington, D.C.

"Looking is not as simple as it looks," said Ad Reinhardt in 1946. And he went on to prove it with a long series of paintings which culminated in the black paintings of which this is one. It takes time and patience to decipher the cruciform image which lies within the matt, light-absorbing surface of the canvas; but Reinhardt's intention was to free the observer from the conventional time-span within which we look at art. A lifelong polemicist, cartoonist, demonstrator and writer of enraged letters on subjects that were dear to him, Reinhardt in his late paintings aimed at a terminal statement: a point beyond which easel painting could go no further. And in his own terms, in paintings such as this one, he achieved it.

19. Jim Dine
Five Feet of Colorful Tools, 1962
The Museum of Modern Art, New York

Dine's father and grandfather were store-
keepers and he grew to regard the
hammer, the C-clamp, the saw, the wooden
mallet, the pair of pliers, the screwdriver
and the vise as his predestined com-
panions. He learned to draw them superlatively well, and he also learned in time
to use them just as they were. They formed
up (as here) as part-sculpture, part-relief;
and Dine used paint and canvas to
integrate them into a severe, formal
composition.

tive example were an inspiration to artists who wanted to get more and more of the world into their art. In 1958 this point was put by Allan Kaprow, artist and theoretician, when he wrote that "Pollock left us at the point where we must become preoccupied with and even dazzled by the space and objects of our everyday life. . . . Not satisfied with the *suggestion* through paint of other senses, we shall utilize the specific substances of sight, sound, people, movement, odors, touch. Objects of every sort are the material for the new art."

It was in this belief that from 1954 onward art made raid after raid into territory which it had traditionally disdained. The great divide grew ever wider between those who believed, with Thomas B. Hess, that the only art worth talking about was "diffi-cult, serious, remote, aristocratic" and those who believed that, no matter where the action was, art should get a piece of it. The two points of view looked to be irreconcilable, and many of the participants were determined that they should remain so. "Avoid a polar situation," Johns had said: but what common ground could there be between Ad Reinhardt, who said that "a museum is a treasure house and a tomb, not a countinghouse or an amuse-ment center," and Claes Oldenburg, who said that he was for "an art which did something else but sit on its ass in a museum"?

23

20. Roy Lichtenstein
Girl with Ball, 1961
Philip Johnson, New Canaan, Conn.

21. Roy Lichtenstein
Diana, 1965
Mr. and Mrs. Leo Castelli, New York

22. Roy Lichtenstein
George Washington, 1962
Mr. and Mrs. Ned Owyang, New York

The source material here was an advertisement for vacations in the Poconos. Lichtenstein introduced into the painting allusions both to the technology of printing (the benday dots which serve as skin tone for the vacationing girl) and to the recent history of art (the curvilinear Art Nouveau forms which designate her hair, the cropping of the whole image at top and bottom to bring it closer to the spectator, and the firmly drawn line which unites the profile of the wave to the outline of the girl's body). What looks crude and simplistic to eyes nurtured on French Impressionism results in reality from a series of conscious and intelligent decisions.

Roy Lichtenstein in the early 1960s probed one after another the kinds of image we acknowledge, cherish, or in some cases have simply got used to and no longer notice. One such was the likeness of George Washington as it turns up over and over again in post-Colonial times. Another was the stylized notion of gods and goddesses: the cameo portrait, in this case, of a fabled queen and huntress.

THE RATIONALE OF POP ART

The truth is that by the mid-1950s too much new energy had come into everyday life, and too many new forms of awareness were available to the artist, for any but the most steadfast of gifted natures to look neither to right nor to left. What Reinhardt called "Art-as-something-else" was irresistibly attractive when the world as it had previously existed was turning out to be obsolete and new ways of life were calling out for comment. Reinhardt stood, on the contrary, for what he called "Art-as-only-itself." In May, 1957, he wrote that "the first rule and absolute standard of fine art, and of painting, which is the highest and freest art, is the purity of it. The more uses, relations, and "additions" a painting has, the less pure it is. The more stuff in it, the busier the work of art, the worse it is. More is Less."

Reinhardt himself acted on these principles, with an ever-growing stringency, till his death in 1967. One or two others, as

23. (*left*) George Segal
The Butcher Shop,
1965
Art Gallery of
Ontario, Toronto

24. Berenice Abbott
*New York Shop-
front,* c. 1936–37
Museum of the City
of New York

George Segal's *The Butcher Shop* has a hieratic, abstract quality—a feeling for ritual on an almost bare stage—which is in striking contrast to Berenice Abbott's photograph of the real thing as it was in the 1930s. The Segal has the look of classical drama; the Abbott—one of many in which she recorded a New York now largely vanished—has a Dickensian delight in detail.

we shall see, did the same and are still doing it with a singular scorn for compromise. Sometimes superb work resulted, with a critical follow-up remarkable for both cogency and conviction: the thing written and the thing done were one, almost. But the work that got itself talked about by laymen in the 1960s originated for the most part in what Rauschenberg had called the gap between art and life; and it overturned three of Thomas B. Hess's requirements by being not remote, not difficult, and not aristocratic. (Whether it was not serious would have to be debated case by case.) At the highest level there were points of contact—Johns and Noland both painted targets, as I said earlier, and the panoramic and environmental scale of Action Painting was common both among Pop painters (James Rosenquist, above all) and among sculptors of several persuasions (Louise Nevelson, George Segal)—but fundamentally the great divide was never deeper or wider than in the 1960s.

If the world can be thought of as one gigantic painting, as Rauschenberg had suggested in 1961, it follows that we can cut into it almost at random and come up with something that hangs together as art. "If I call it art, it's art," had been the implication of what Marcel Duchamp did when he signed a urinal in 1917 and sent it in for an exhibition. Pop art (as it came to be called) did not quite do that; its impact was owed to the combination of unprocessed material from everyday life with traditional fine art procedures (paint on canvas, adjustments of scale, adroit reemphasis, and the use of isolated details in the interest of irony or pathos). In fact it claimed for itself the privileges (and, eventually, the financial rewards) of high art, while sticking closely to subject matter with which high art had never associated before. "To think that I have been speaking prose all my life and never knew it!" says Monsieur Jourdain in Molière's *Le Bourgeois Gentilhomme;* in the same way, people learned from Andy Warhol and Roy

25

VI. Roy Lichtenstein
M-Maybe, 1965
Wallraf-Richartz-Museum, Cologne

VII. Kenneth Noland
Bend Sinister, 1964
The Hirshhorn Museum and Sculpture Garden, Smithsonian Institution,
   Washington, D.C.

25. Larry Rivers
Study for *George Washington Crossing the Delaware,* 1953
The Museum of Modern Art, New York

26. Larry Rivers
Study for *George Washington Crossing the Delaware,* 1953
The Museum of Modern Art, New York

Rivers is a very gifted draftsman who in earlier days took an intense pleasure in copying drawings by Leonardo da Vinci, Dürer and others. In preparing his idiosyncratic reworking of Leutze's famous *Washington Crossing the Delaware* he made drawing after drawing which have a rare sense of immediacy; history is relived in them, and not merely mimicked.

Larry Rivers has always liked to take an outright masterpiece from the past of art and feel his way back toward it by an unexpected route. He has done this with the Dutch 17th-century masters by way of a familiar brand of cigars, and with Japanese painting by way of a child's coloring book. In this case he paid homage to Cézanne's *The Card Players* by way of a commemorative stamp.

27. Larry Rivers
Cézanne Stamp, 1963
The Hirshhorn Museum and Sculpture Garden, Smithsonian Institution,
    Washington, D.C.

Lichtenstein that they had lived among art all their lives and never known it.

There was more to Pop art than this, however—and more, too, to the exasperation of those who could not abide it. Pop art had complex motives. One of them was to see just how far it could flout the expectations of the "cultivated" public (Roy Lichtenstein said that his ambition had been to produce a picture so hideous that no one would hang it). What was put to the test was the automatic reverence, the white flag of immunity from comment, which is accorded to the large framed painting *as such,* no matter how bitterly the status of individual paintings may be contested.

Next came an important social change, and one not yet definitively acknowledged. Generation after generation had taken for granted that the categories proposed by the novelist Sinclair Lewis in his *Babbitt* (1922) were eternal and unchangeable. They believed that there was such a thing as the cultivated life, on the one hand, and that on the other hand there was life as it was led by the vast majority of Americans. That majority was discounted as mediocre, undiscriminating, herd-minded, all but illiterate. One of the best things that ever happened to America is that between 1950 and 1970 this idea got a thorough going-over and was to a large degree discredited. Of course there were still plenty of Babbitts around; but there was a new self-awareness on the part of other generations, and one of the rewards of this was the realization that there is such a thing as popular culture and that it is primarily in relation to the popular culture of the day that each generation defines itself. Anyone who happened to read J. D. Salinger's *The Catcher in the Rye* on the day of its publication in 1951 will have recognized not only the portrait of a new archetypal young American but the arrival of a new attitude to popular culture. Popular culture from that day onward was neither something to be over-inflated, in fan-club style, nor something to be put down by set-faced heads of families: it was just *there*, once and for all, as a complete structure in relation to which young people could find out who they were.

Pop art had its place in all this. It was also one of its functions to de-mystify the procedures of fine art. One of the monuments of Pop is George Segal's *The Butcher Shop*, 1965 (fig. 23)—a reconstruction, as it happens, of the shop owned by Segal's father: the locus, therefore, of his deepest and earliest intimations of how life is carried on from one day to the next. *The Butcher Shop* has the stillness of the image of an ancient Greek stele, but it is also direct, immediate and actual in a way that is akin to the black-and-white movies of Segal's youth. It is of yesterday, but it is also of all time. It speaks for the ancient ritual by which we take life so that we ourselves may survive: but it has none of the stylization with which the sculptors of the 19th century hoped to make their work last forever. A complete society is somewhere there inside it, and yet it is made up of plaster casts and a summary architecture, with no pretensions to high art.

There was in Pop art an element of exorcism. It was made to banish evil memories, or to hoist them to a level on which they would lose their power to degrade. Segal's father, in effigy, has a dignity which society did not always accord him in life. Robert Indiana's numerals have none of the philosophical implications

28. Andy Warhol
Electric Chair, 1966
Institute for the Arts, Rice University, Houston, Texas

of Johns's; they are based on the memory of a time when the great numbered highways of the United States meant the possibility of escape from the grinding meanness of life in the Depression. James Rosenquist's *F-111* (pl. VIII; fig. 29) puts as cogently as anyone could wish the case against the uses to which the American Air Force was beginning to be put; "If I spell it out large enough," he seems to say, "someone's going to read it." It is more difficult to ascribe any one motive to Andy Warhol, since Warhol operates behind a mask of inarticulacy, but his Electric Chair (fig. 28) and his Car Crash series undoubtedly reminded people of what was being done in their name, in the one case, and of what they may well end up doing themselves, in the other. In the Happenings pioneered by Jim Dine, Claes Oldenburg and Allan Kaprow in 1959–60 there was, equally, a strong element of social protest.

Much in all this was subject before long to what the poet and novelist James Agee called "the emasculation of acceptance." It was difficult to sustain that point of maximum tension—fundamental to the creation of a valid art—between what needs to be said and the means which are available for saying it. "Don't bother with that. Just do it all over again" is the message of the market; and it was difficult in the mid-1960s to recapture the élan which powered Pop art when Claes Oldenburg hired a real store

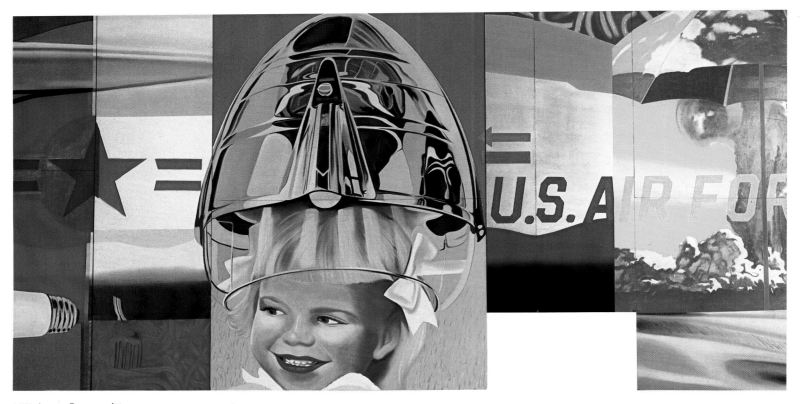

VIII. James Rosenquist
F-111 (partial view), 1965
Mr. and Mrs. Robert C. Scull, New York

With his panoramic *F-111* James Rosenquist renewed the tradition of outrage which had produced Picasso's *Guernica* (Volume 9), and Miró's *Head of a Woman* (Volume 7). The picture is polemical in intent; and it suggests, among much else, that something is wrong with a world in which the production of a new kind of aircraft allows one little girl to sit laughing under the hair-dryer while other little girls in a distant country will be burnt to death when that same aircraft gets into service.

to sell his simulated pieces of pie. It was a time for evolution. Sometimes the evolution was merely toward the tactics of merchandising; in such cases the moral thrust of the work quite withered away.

Sometimes, on the other hand, it turned out that artists had been double agents for high art all the time. Jasper Johns, for one—though never a Pop artist in any strict sense—had been the source of much that was later taken over from him by other artists in simplified form, and when he produced his *Painted Bronze* (fig. 32) in 1960 many people took it as an affront: the *Bed* all over again. How could two beer cans be art? Surely it was all part of a wager? (Someone had said of Johns's dealer, Leo Castelli, that "that so-and-so could sell beer cans as art if he put his mind to it.") People who went to see the work itself before making up their minds soon realized that the two cans had their place in

29. James Rosenquist
F-111, 1965
Mr. and Mrs. Robert C. Scull, New York

high art, as securely as did Picasso's *Glass of Absinthe* (Volume 4), so clear at every point was the mark of Johns's governing hand. It turned out, equally, that Roy Lichtenstein was as capable of working from Monet's Cathedrals, or from his Haystack series, as from the comic strips which had made his name. As for the direct reproduction of objects of common use—well, it was plain to any unprejudiced person that Alex Hay's aggrandizement in paper, epoxy, fiberglass and paint of an E-ze brown paper bag, done in 1968 (fig. 36), was one of the most elegant of art objects and not at all the put-on that it would have been assumed to be ten years earlier.

The great divide was in no way narrowed, however, by the fact that Reinhardt's "Art-as-only-itself" had infiltrated the enemy camp. These incidents were thought of, indeed, as gross improprieties. Historical allusions had at most a parasitic function: a

play element quite out of place in serious art. As to that, a firm opinion was forthcoming from the Viennese-born philosopher Ludwig Wittgenstein, whose later books were required reading for all ambitious people in the 1960s (not least for those whose first and last experience of philosophy they were). Wittgenstein had said that "something new (spontaneous, 'specific') is always a language game"; and this was in line with the general trend of fashionable thought in the 1960s, when linguistics was all the rage in the paperback bookshops.

Play has, however, a quality of reaching outward. Play is a dramatization of our deepest concerns. In play, we mime the strategies for survival which are so fundamental to our equilibrium that we dare not reveal them in any other way. Chess, tennis, golf, baseball, football in its various guises—all serve to externalize our anxieties. ("No chess playing" was one of Ad

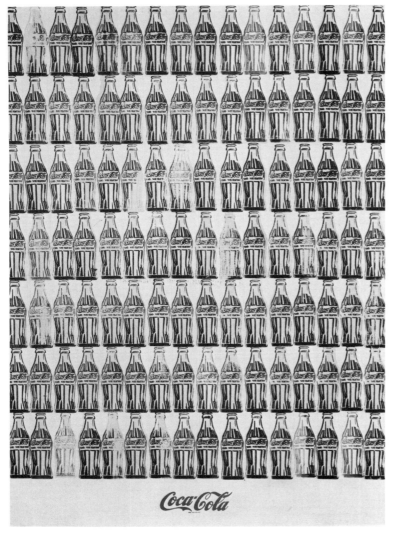

30. Andy Warhol
Green Coca-Cola Bottles, 1962
Whitney Museum of American Art, New York

Where Jasper Johns in *Numbers in Color* (pl.IV) renews the great tradition of oil painting with reference to a subject which might seem entirely impersonal, Warhol with his Coca-Cola bottles aims, rather, at the effect of a print-run that is not quite perfect. It is with what would elsewhere be called errors of registration that he sustains our interest from row to serried row.

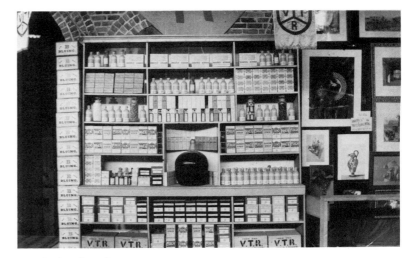

31. Charles Ellis Johnson
Druggist's Display, Featuring Valley Tan Remedy, 1888
Jonathan L. Fairbanks, Boston

Insistent repetition of the kind used by Warhol in his *Green Coca-Cola Bottles* (fig. 30) is a perennial feature of American life. In this photograph of a provincial druggist's shop in the year 1888 the same principle is applied to canker syrup, essence of ginger, "Essence of Life" and an all-purpose medicine called the "Valley Tan Remedy."

32. Jasper Johns
Painted Bronze, 1960
The Ludwig Collection, on loan to the Kunstmuseum, Basel, Switzerland

34. (*right*) Claes Oldenburg
Soft Juicit, 1965
Courtesy Blum/Helman Gallery,
   New York

33. Claes Oldenburg
Soft Manhattan #1 (Postal Zones),
   1966
Albright-Knox Art Gallery,
   Buffalo, N.Y.

Oldenburg here takes the zip code map of Manhattan, as it appears at the beginning of the telephone directory, and builds it up, block by block, as a sculpture, with the tall thin shape of Central Park conspicuous in the center. We become conscious as never before of the interlocked segments which make up a mailman's Manhattan; and the piece also works as a work of art, to be hung from a nail on the wall and quizzed, day after day, for what it has to offer.

With vinyl, kapok and fake fur Claes Oldenburg produced a sculpture which is two things in one. It is the portrait of the way a juicer might look if it melted like wax while halfway through juicing an orange. And it is a self-portrait of the artist himself, complete with cap, a few strands of untidy fair hair, a half-hidden face, and what might be a parka several sizes too big for him.

Reinhardt's rules and regulations for a new art.) When Jasper Johns wanted to emphasize that the painter is the prisoner of a perfectly flat surface which can only be concealed by obsolete make-believe, he put a real drawer, complete with knobs, in the middle of the picture. But this was a device from outside of art, and as such unacceptable to those who believed that high art must ensure its continuance within the terms of its own physical existence and in no other way.

Clement Greenberg was an embattled supporter of this point of view, and what he had to say is worth quoting at length. He saw the predicament of art in the late 1950s and '60s as a part of a historical process that had begun with the German philosopher Immanuel Kant. It was by self-criticism that art survived; and around the beginning of our century, at a time when many of art's prerogatives were being taken away, a process of radical self-criticism began. The survival of art would depend on the thoroughness with which artists defined the areas in which art could still do incomparably well.

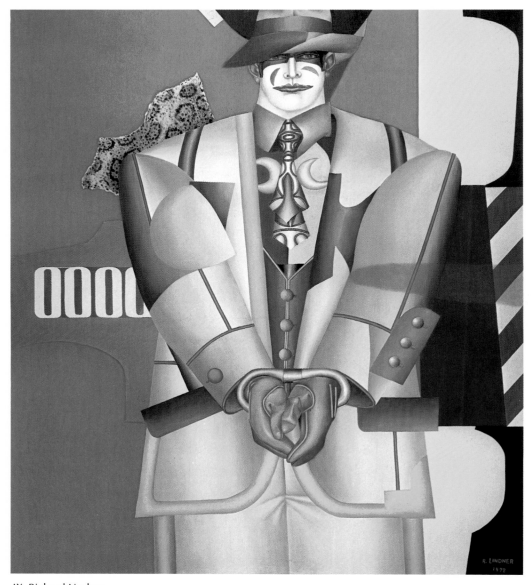

IX. Richard Lindner
East 69th Street, 1972
Museum Boymans-van Beuningen, Rotterdam

For some years Richard Lindner lived on East 69th Street in New York City. His apartment was only a few doors away from the headquarters of the F.B.I.; and Lindner was much taken with the idea that on his very own street tabs were being kept on the mobsters and hoodlums in whom he had taken a lifelong and an immensely sardonic interest. *East 69th Street* has to do with the imagined arrest of a king of the Underworld, a kid-gloved Lucifer for whom only the newest and most stylish men's wear will do. It has the relish with which George Grosz and Bertolt Brecht would seize on people of the same sort; but it also has a flat heraldic quality which is one of Lindner's contributions to the American painting of our day.

X. Claes Oldenburg
Pastry Case, I, 1961–62
The Museum of Modern Art, New York

35. Richard Hamilton
Just What Is It That Makes Today's Homes So Different, So Appealing? 1956
Private collection, Tübingen, Germany

Within this tiny image (fig. 35) Richard Hamilton inventorized as early as 1956
the themes which were to nourish Pop art over the next ten years: the comic
strip, the billboard, the movie still, the commercialized exploitation of sex, the
ransacked ads, the references to up-to-the-minute technology. It was all there,
together with a wry, offhand wit which is Hamilton's own.

37. Richard Hamilton
I'm Dreaming of a White Christmas, 1967
Courtesy Petersburg Press, New York and London

Hamilton has always been fascinated by the film still and, even more so, by the
single frame that does not normally have an independent existence. Given an
image of that kind, he dredges it for its immediate emotional impact—the
memory, in this case, both of a once-inescapable popular song and of the
troubadour who made it famous—and for the possibilities of metamorphosis
which it may offer. This particular glimpse of Bing Crosby at his most easy-
going was worked and reworked a hundred times over—both in Hamilton's
own studio and in the workshops of specialized printers in Hamburg and
Stuttgart—and turned out to yield virtually unlimited opportunities for
restatement and reconstitution.

IN SEARCH OF THE IRREDUCIBLE

"What had to be made explicit," Greenberg wrote, "was that which was unique and irreducible not only in art in general but also in each particular art. Each art had to determine, through the operations peculiar to itself, the effects peculiar and exclusive to itself. By doing this, each art, would, to be sure, narrow its area of competence, but at the same time it would make its possession of this area all the more secure."

"It quickly emerged," Greenberg went on, "that the unique and proper area of competence of each art coincided with all that was unique to the nature of its medium. The task of self-criticism became to eliminate from the effects of each art any and every effect that might conceivably be borrowed from or by the medium of any other art. Thereby each art would be rendered 'pure,' and in its 'purity' find the guarantee of its standards of quality as well as of its independence. 'Purity' meant self-definition, and the enterprise of self-criticism in the arts became one of self-definition with a vengeance."

Whether or not Greenberg was aware of the overtones of the word "vengeance" in this context, the program that he set out had undeniably a punitive quality. Old scores were to be settled, old wrongs put right, sham heroes toppled from their pedestals, and the one true faith upheld. Good art—or "strong art," as it was called—was to be made within a set of conditions that grew ever more stringent until eventually everything that was not prohibited would be mandatory. One of the things to be said about all this is that it actually worked: good art and strong art were made, year by year, on the basis of a reductive program, a series of logical and ruthless decisions, that concentrated on the essential practicalities of art: the size and shape of the stretcher, the physical characteristics of the paint, the extent to which the final image was free from the taint of illusionism.

Fundamental to all this was the role of color. Color had been set free, as we all know, by 1914. But was there such a thing as freer than free? The dying Matisse proved that there was, with the cut-paper paintings that he had produced in 1950–53. But those paintings were still not well known, and they were in any case a function of terminal illness, on the one hand, and of 60 years of research on the other. The problem was to make color freer than free as a logical next step forward from what had been done by Mark Rothko, for one, in America. It could be done, and it was done to stunning effect by Kenneth Noland in paintings like *Bend Sinister* (p VII). In the sideways thrust of that colossal image (it measures 7 feet 8 inches by 13 feet 5 inches) it seems as if color, incorporeal and unsupported, were pulling itself free

38. Kenneth Noland
Beginning, 1958
The Hirshhorn Museum and Sculpture Garden, Smithsonian Institution, Washington, D.C.

from the absolute flatness: with just one unprecedented heave, the thing was done.

When seen by itself, *Bend Sinister* impresses by the authority with which a unified and seemingly quite simple image is made to carry the whole burden of art. It is even more arresting, however, if we know the paintings which immediately preceded it: chevron images which hang down with a perfect symmetry, blasting off from the two top corners of the canvas and hurtling straight on down toward the exact center of the canvas's lower edge. These centered chevrons have an added meaning, in their turn, if we know what came before *them*: and so on back to the beginning of Noland's career.

Even then, we need to know more: for Noland is one of the painters who bear out van Gogh's prediction that no one man could bring the art of the future into being. It would have to be done, van Gogh thought, by groups or teams, or at the very least by paired enthusiasts (like Gauguin and himself in their more

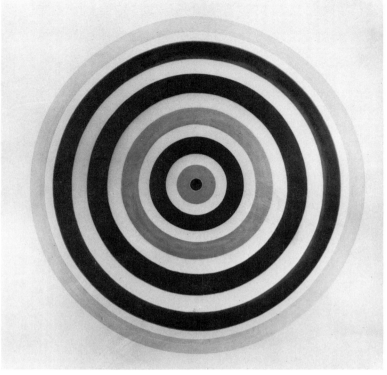

39. Kenneth Noland
Plus 10, 1964
Dr. and Mrs. Joseph A. Gosman, Toledo, Ohio

40. Kenneth Noland
Reverberations, 1961
Mr. and Mrs. John G. Powers, New York

harmonious days). Van Gogh was proved right by the history of subsequent art, in which not one consequential movement has been the work of a man on his own. Bonnard and Vuillard; Matisse, Derain, Vlaminck; Picasso and Braque; Kirchner and his friends in Dresden; Kandinsky and his friends in Munich; Lunacharsky's protégés in the U.S.S.R.; the Dadaists and the Surrealists in their heyday—in every case there was a collective impulse. How it was in New York in the 1940s we have seen; and although it is easy to exaggerate the degree of complicity which joins one coeval to another there is no doubt that in the 1950s the friendship of Kenneth Noland with Morris Louis, and to a lesser extent with the sculptor David Smith, was fundamental to the development of American art.

Louis and Noland met in 1952 in Washington, D.C., where they both lived. Morris Louis was by 12 years the older of the

two, but it was Noland who had the kind of outgoing, combative temperament which thrives on the definition of ideas: and for the three years—1952–55—of their close friendship they were able to effect a joint hammering-out of their intentions such as had rarely been paralleled since the first alliance of Picasso and Braque. (At one time they even painted on the same canvas.)

What were they doing? Well, they wanted to find out what was the predestined next thing in art: the step which history dictated, but which it was left to individual men and women to riddle out. As friends of Clement Greenberg, they proceeded by elimination: by defining their "area of competence," no matter how narrow it might turn out to be. Noland had spent some time at Black Mountain College as a student of the Russian-born painter Ilya Bolotowsky, who brought to his raw young audiences something of the European abstract tradition. He had

XI. Andy Warhol
Numbers, 1962
Mr. and Mrs. Bagley Wright, Seattle

Warhol was always interested in the de-mystification of art: in its reduction, in other words, to something that at first glance could be done by anyone. This adaptation of a do-it-yourself painting manual is a particularly crisp and jaunty example; and it is one of the many paradoxes of Warhol's career that this image should be so inescapably his own.

41. Helen Frankenthaler
Mountains and Sea, 1952
Collection the artist, New York

worked in Paris, where the sculptor Ossip Zadkine (then one of the most famous artists in Europe) had singled him out in 1949 as someone of exceptional promise. Noland had steam up, by the end of the 1940s, but he had nowhere to go—until, that is, he and Morris Louis began to work on the impressions they had brought back from Helen Frankenthaler's studio in 1953. In her *Mountains and Sea* (fig. 41) they found an answer to the question "What is it that art can still do, *and that nothing else can?*" In

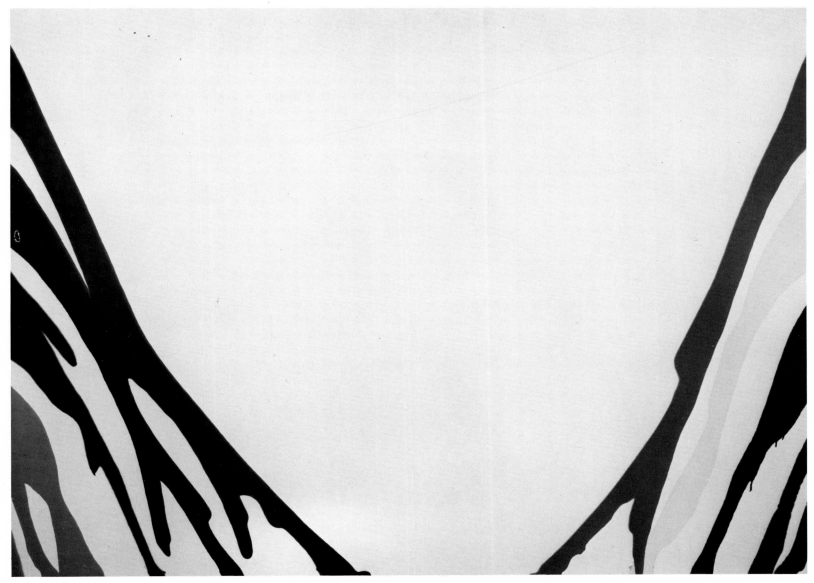

42. Morris Louis
Alpha Gamma, 1960
The Detroit Institute of Arts

Toward the end of his short life Morris Louis allowed runnels of pure color to stream diagonally across the corners of a very large canvas which was elsewhere left blank. As much as in the paintings of Matisse before 1914, color was set free by this device. Pure, autonomous and uncontaminated, it went its own way; we remember how the poet Percy Bysshe Shelley once likened life to "a dome of many-colored glass, staining the white radiance of eternity."

paintings like *Mountains and Sea* and *Other Generations* (pl. II) Frankenthaler in the 1950s was onto something all her own: the alliance of delicate freehand drawing with paint that was allowed to stain its way into the canvas rather than to sit, like a skin, on top of it. Hers was not the only answer: Matisse and Braque in France had lately come upon quite different ones, for instance. But it was an answer that they followed through to spectacular effect: Louis until he died in 1962, Noland to this day.

XII. Morris Louis
Point of Tranquillity, 1958
The Hirshhorn Museum and Sculpture Garden, Smithsonian Institution,
  Washington, D.C.

42

43. Frank Stella
The Marriage of Reason and Squalor, 1959
The Museum of Modern Art, New York

After a decade and more when the subjectivity of Abstract Expressionism had dominated the New York art scene, it was Frank Stella, above all, who put the case for quite another kind of painting: one in which the image would be "given," centered, symmetrical and invariable.

Certain things were eliminated from the start, as having lately exhausted their usefulness. One of them was the manual element in painting: the evident motion of the hand, whether with brush or tube or can, which left its mark on the canvas in the form of motor energy. Another was drawing, in any of its accepted forms, since anything that could be read as drawing could also be read as illusion, or as metaphor: the pounding rhythms of a major abstract Pollock demand, for instance, to be described in terms of loops and skeins and lassoes. A third thing to be eliminated was composition, as it was generally understood; for composi-

43

tion in Action Painting as often as not looked back to composition as it had evolved in Cubist painting, even down to the uneasiness which seized the Cubist painters as they got further and further from the closely argued central image and had to decide what to do at the edges of the canvas.

So a lot was going out. What was coming in? New ways of applying paint, to begin with: after that, new ways of structuring the image. Thinned pigment (the new synthetic paint called "acrylic") was to be soaked and stained into unsized canvas. Instead of building up on the surface of the canvas, in traditional style, the paint sank into the canvas and became one with it. Just how this was to be done—how the artist was to govern the nature of the image without being seen to direct it—was a matter for discussion. The paint could be poured onto a canvas laid flat on the floor; it could be allowed to run down a canvas that was held up as one holds up a sheet for folding; it could be rubbed in with a sponge; and it could be rolled on with a commercial paint roller. The important thing was that none of the traditional signs of "handling" should be present: no mark should be seen to result from a strong forward movement of the arm, a turn of the wrist, a well-judged dab with the brush held between two fingers and thumb. Color should seem to act spontaneously and of its own nature.

As to the structuring of the image, Louis and Noland proceeded according to their own very different natures. Louis was physically frail, and by temperament he was a quiet, inward sort of person. Noland liked to bring everything into the open, and to go to work from a position of armored certainty. Louis at more than one stage of his career echoed the aspirations of the American sublime; Noland did not want overtones of any kind, anywhere. In a top class Morris Louis—in one of the "unfurled" paintings, for instance—color seems to go its own way, freer than ever before or since, down runnels which are never the same twice over. In a top class Kenneth Noland, we know who's boss, down to the last millimeter of the surface. Louis did not exclude a monumental ambiguity—above all, in the Veils series in 1954, and again in 1958—but a mature Noland is a statement-system in which clear thoughts find clear expression and there is never a conflict of intention, never a second thought, never an evocative fuzz. As much as Picasso and Braque, the two artists complement one another.

The American critic Michael Fried put the case for this when he said that "only an art of constant formal self-criticism can bear or embody or communicate more than trivial meaning." The self-criticism which he had in mind was limited to a very few areas of investigation. These were (i) the echoes or implications of the picture's physical format, (ii) the avoidance of anything that could be likened to freehand drawing, (iii) the nature of a specifically post-Cubist composition, (iv) the extent to which color could be given, not "freedom," but a total independence. These were severe prescriptions; and if we consider the area of competence which until quite recently was taken for granted in art there is no doubt that in the 1960s the field of permissible effort was dramatically narrowed. "On this ground," these painters and their friends seem to say, "painting will make its last stand."

There is here something of American folklore. The ghost of General Custer, face to face with Crazy Horse, comes over the horizon; and, with him, something of the first settlers' determination to build a new world, a Jerusalem untainted by the falling-short of their forebears in Europe. Plain talking and plain doing were the remedy: and we seem to hear an echo of those days when Frank Stella suggests in his black paintings of 1960 that thereafter the only defensible basis for composition is the shape and size of the wooden battens on which the canvas has been stretched. There is, too, that same delight in exact measurement which, as we have seen, was identified by Emerson in the 1830s as a specifically American trait. Literal truth is fundamental to this kind of painting; and the implication is that as long as painting sticks with literal truth it can never be dislodged from its functions. When trueing and fairing are mentioned in connection with these pictures, we remember that "true" and "fair" bear a moral as much as a physical connotation.

The work which results from all this could be dull and schematic, well-argued but unfeeling. So much is outlawed that was once among the painter's most valued prerogatives: allusion, ambiguity, freedom of reference, the right to establish ideal standards of beauty both in human beings and in Nature, and the power to make changes of pace and tone and intent within one and the same picture. It is a tribute to the artists whose work is reproduced here that they have been able, nonetheless, to make feeling flow where none flowed before. With a chevron, a set of immensely elongated stripes, or five or six batons of pure color laid side by side, Louis and Noland have given back to painting a purity and an intensity of feeling such as we needed but did not dare to hope could still exist. What more natural than that those who have experienced this need most acutely should feel that there and there only lies the salvation of art? Between them, on the one hand, are those who claim for art an altogether wider set of options, on the other, no compromise is possible. The great divide has never been wider; nor could the art of this generation tread more consistently on tender ground.

SELECTED READINGS

American Art

Amaya, Mario. *Pop Art . . . And After.*
  New York, Viking, 1965.

Battcock, Gregory, ed. *The New Art.*
  New York, E. P. Dutton, 1966.

Cage, John. *A Year from Monday: New Lectures and Writings.*
  Middletown, Conn., Wesleyan University Press, 1967.

Geldzahler, Henry. *American Painting of the Twentieth Century.*
  New York, The Metropolitan Museum of Art, 1965.

Geldzahler, Henry. *New York Painting and Sculpture: 1940–1970.*
  New York, The Metropolitan Museum of Art, 1969.

Greenberg, Clement. *Art and Culture: Critical Essays.*
  Boston, Beacon Press, 1961.

Hunter, Sam, and Jacobus, John. *American Art of the 20th Century: Painting, Sculpture and Architecture.*
  New York, Abrams, 1974.

Kramer, Hilton. *The Age of the Avant-Garde: An Art Chronicle of 1956–1972.*
  New York, Farrar, Straus and Giroux, 1973.

Kuh, Katharine, ed. *The Artist's Voice.*
  New York, Harper and Row, 1962.

Lippard, Lucy. *Pop Art.*
  New York, Praeger, 1966.

O'Hara, Frank. *Art Chronicles, 1954–1966.*
  New York, Braziller, 1975.

Rose, Barbara. *American Art Since 1900: A Critical History.* Revised edition.
  (World of Art ser.)
  New York, Praeger, 1975.

Russell, John, and Gablik, Suzi. *Pop Art Redefined.*
  New York, Praeger, 1969.

Seitz, William C. *The Art of Assemblage.*
  New York, The Museum of Modern Art, 1961.

Steinberg, Leo. *Other Criteria: Confrontations with Twentieth-Century Art.*
  New York, Oxford University Press, 1972.

Helen Frankenthaler

Rose, Barbara. *Frankenthaler.*
  New York, Abrams, 1972.

Jasper Johns

Kozloff, Max. *Jasper Johns.*
  New York, Abrams, 1969.

Steinberg, Leo. *Jasper Johns.*
  New York, Wittenborn, 1963.

Franz Kline

Dawson, Fielding. *An Emotional Memoir of Franz Kline.*
  New York, Pantheon, 1967.

Roy Lichtenstein

Coplans, John, ed. *Roy Lichtenstein.*
  (Documentary Monographs in Modern Art ser.)
  New York, Praeger, 1972.

Waldman, Diane. *Roy Lichtenstein.*
  New York, Abrams, 1971.

Waldman, Diane. *Roy Lichtenstein: Drawings and Prints.*
  New York, Chelsea House, 1969.

Richard Lindner

Dore, Ashton. *Richard Lindner.*
  New York, Abrams, 1969.

Morris Louis

Fried, Michael. *Morris Louis.*
  New York, Abrams, 1969.

Louise Nevelson

Glimcher, Arnold B. *Louise Nevelson.*
  New York, Praeger, 1972.

Barnett Newman

Hess, Thomas B. *Barnett Newman.*
  New York, Walker, 1969.

Hess, Thomas B. *Barnett Newman.*
  New York, The Museum of Modern Art, 1971.

Claes Oldenburg

Baro, Gene. *Claes Oldenburg: Drawings and Prints.*
  New York, Chelsea House, 1969.

Oldenburg, Claes. *Store Days.*
  New York, Something Else Press, 1967.

Oldenburg, Claes. *Injun and Other Histories.*
  New York, Something Else Press, 1967.

Rose, Barbara. *Claes Oldenburg.*
  New York, The Museum of Modern Art, 1969.

Jackson Pollock

O'Hara, Frank. *Jackson Pollock.* (Great American Artists ser.)
  New York, Braziller, 1959.

Robertson, Bryan. *Jackson Pollock.*
  New York, Abrams, 1960.

Robert Rauschenberg

Forge, Andrew. *Robert Rauschenburg.*
  New York, Abrams, 1972.

Larry Rivers

Hunter, Sam. *Larry Rivers.*
  New York, Abrams, 1969.

George Segal

Seitz, William C. *Segal.*
  New York, Abrams, 1972.

Frank Stella

Rosenblum, Robert. *Frank Stella.* (New Art ser.)
  London and New York, Penguin Books, 1970.

Rubin, William S. *Frank Stella.*
  New York, The Museum of Modern Art, 1970.

Andy Warhol

Coplans, John. *Andy Warhol.*
  Greenwich, Conn., New York Graphic Society, 1970.

Crone, Rainer. *Andy Warhol.*
  New York, Praeger, 1970.

Warhol, Andy. *Andy Warhol's Index Book.*
  New York, Random House, 1967.

LIST OF ILLUSTRATIONS

Dimensions: height precedes width; another dimension, depth, is given for sculptures and constructions where relevant. Foreign titles are in English, except in cases where the title does not translate or is better known in its original form. Asterisked titles indicate works reproduced in color.

Abbott, Berenice
(b. 1898)

New York Shopfront, c. 1936–37 (fig. 24)
Photograph
Museum of the City of New York

Demuth, Charles Henry
(1883–1935)

I Saw the Figure Five in Gold, 1928 (fig. 15)
Oil on composition board, 36 x 29¾ inches
The Metropolitan Museum of Art, New York
The Alfred Stieglitz Collection, 1949

Dine, Jim
(b. 1935)

Five Feet of Colorful Tools, 1962 (fig. 19)
Oil on canvas, surmounted by a board on which
  32 tools hang from hooks, overall:
  55⅝ x 60¼ x 4⅜ inches
The Museum of Modern Art, New York
The Sidney and Harriet Janis Collection

Frankenthaler, Helen
(b. 1928)

Mountains and Sea, 1952 (fig. 41)
Oil on canvas, 7 feet 2⅜ inches x 9 feet 9¼
  inches
Collection the artist, New York

* *Other Generations,* 1957 (pl. II)
Oil on canvas, 70 x 70 inches
Collection the artist, New York

Hamilton, Richard
(b. 1922)

*Just What Is It That Makes Today's Homes So
  Different, So Appealing?* 1956 (fig. 35)
Collage, 10¼ x 9¾ inches
Private collection, Tübingen, Germany

I'm Dreaming of a White Christmas, 1967 (fig. 37)
Screenprint (edition of 75), 30 x 41 inches
Courtesy Petersburg Press, New York and London

Hay, Alex
(b. 1930)

Paper Bag, 1968 (fig. 36)
Fiberglas, epoxy, paint and paper, 59½ x 29 x 18
  inches
Whitney Museum of American Art, New York
Gift of the Friends of the Whitney Museum of
  American Art

Johns, Jasper
(b. 1930)

* *Flag,* 1954 (pl. V)
Encaustic on newsprint over canvas mounted on
  plywood, 42¼ x 60½ inches
The Museum of Modern Art, New York
Gift of Philip Johnson in honor of
  Alfred H. Barr, Jr.

Target with Four Faces, 1955 (fig. 6)
Encaustic on newspaper on canvas surmounted
    by 4 tinted plaster faces in wooden box with
    hinged front, overall (with box open):
    33⅝ x 26 x 3 inches
The Museum of Modern Art, New York
Gift of Mr. and Mrs. Robert C. Scull

Figure 5, 1955 (fig. 14)
Encaustic and collage on canvas, 17½ x 14 inches
Collection the artist, New York

White Flag, 1955–58 (fig. 12)
Encaustic and collage on canvas, 52¼ x 78¾
    inches
Mr. and Mrs. Burton Tremaine, Meriden, Conn.

*Numbers in Color, 1959 (pl. IV)
Encaustic and collage on canvas, 66½ x 49½
    inches
Albright-Knox Art Gallery, Buffalo, N.Y.
Gift of Seymour H. Knox

Painted Bronze, 1960 (fig. 32)
Painted bronze, 5½ x 8 x 4¾ inches
The Ludwig Collection, on loan to the
    Kunstmuseum, Basel, Switzerland

Johnson, Charles Ellis
(1857–1926)

Druggist's Display, Featuring Valley Tan Remedy,
    1888 (fig. 31)
Photograph
Jonathan L. Fairbanks, Boston

Kline, Franz
(1910–62)

Painting Number 2, 1954 (fig. 1)
Oil on canvas, 6 feet 8½ inches x 8 feet 9 inches
The Museum of Modern Art, New York
Mr. and Mrs. Joseph H. Hazen and
    Mr. and Mrs. Francis F. Rosenbaum Funds

Lichtenstein, Roy
(b. 1923)

Girl with Ball, 1961 (fig. 20)
Oil on canvas, 60½ x 36½ inches
Philip Johnson, New Canaan, Conn.

George Washington, 1962 (fig. 22)
Pencil and frottage, 18¾ x 14½ inches
Mr. and Mrs. Ned Owyang, New York

Diana, 1965 (fig. 21)
Pencil and tusche on paper, 29¾ x 22¼ inches
Mr. and Mrs. Leo Castelli, New York

*M-Maybe, 1965 (pl. VI)
Oil and magna on canvas, 60 x 60 inches
Wallraf-Richartz-Museum, Cologne
The Ludwig Collection

Lindner, Richard
(b. 1901)

*East 69th Street, 1972 (pl. IX)
Oil on canvas, 80 x 70 inches
Museum Boymans-van Beuningen, Rotterdam

Louis, Morris
(1912–62)

*Point of Tranquillity, 1958 (pl. XII)
Acrylic on canvas, 8 feet 5 inches x 11 feet 3
    inches
The Hirshhorn Museum and Sculpture Garden,
    Smithsonian Institution, Washington, D.C.

Alpha Gamma, 1960 (fig. 42)
Acrylic on canvas, 8 feet 9 inches x 12 feet 1 inch
The Detroit Institute of Arts

Nevelson, Louise
(b. 1900)

Sky Cathedral, 1958 (fig. 17)
Assemblage: wood construction, painted black,
    11 feet 3⅜ inches x 10 feet ¼ inch x 1 foot
    6 inches
The Museum of Modern Art, New York
Gift of Mr. and Mrs. Ben Mildwoff

Newman, Barnett
(1905–70)

Day One, 1951–52 (fig. 2)
Oil on canvas, 11 feet x 4 feet 2¼ inches
Whitney Museum of American Art, New York
Gift of the Friends of the Whitney Museum of
    American Art

Noland, Kenneth
(b. 1924)

Beginning, 1958 (fig. 38)
Acrylic on canvas, 7 feet 6 inches x 8 feet
The Hirshhorn Museum and Sculpture Garden,
    Smithsonian Institution, Washington, D.C.

Flutter, 1960 (fig. 13)
Oil on canvas, 67½ x 68 inches
Mr. and Mrs. Albrecht Saalfield, Bellhaven, Conn.

Reverberations, 1961 (fig. 40)
Oil on canvas, 8 feet x 8 feet
Mr. and Mrs. John G. Powers, New York

*Bend Sinister, 1964 (pl. VII)
Acrylic on canvas, 7 feet 8¾ inches x 13 feet
    5¾ inches
The Hirshhorn Museum and Sculpture Garden,
    Smithsonian Institution, Washington, D.C.

Plus 10, 1964 (fig. 39)
Acrylic resin on canvas, 6 feet x 6 feet
Dr. and Mrs. Joseph A. Gosman, Toledo, Ohio

Oldenburg, Claes
(b. 1929)

*Pastry Case, I, 1961–62 (pl. X)
Enamel paint on nine plaster sculptures in glass
    showcase, 20¾ x 30⅛ x 14¾ inches
The Museum of Modern Art, New York
The Sidney and Harriet Janis Collection

Soft Juicit, 1965 (fig. 34)
Vinyl filled with kapok and fake fur, 21 inches
    high
Courtesy Blum/Helman Gallery, New York

Soft Manhattan #1 (Postal Zones), 1966 (fig. 33)
Stenciled canvas and kapok, 80 x 30 x 8 inches
Albright-Knox Art Gallery, Buffalo, N.Y.
Gift of Seymour H. Knox

Pollock, Jackson
(1912–56)

White Light, 1954 (fig. 4)
Oil, aluminum and enamel paint on canvas,
    48¼ x 38¼ inches
The Museum of Modern Art, New York
The Sidney and Harriet Janis Collection

Rauschenberg, Robert
(b. 1925)

*Charlene, 1954 (pl. I)
Combine painting in 4 sections, 7 feet 5 inches x
    9 feet 4 inches
Stedelijk Museum, Amsterdam

*Bed, 1955 (pl. III)
Combine painting, 74 x 31 inches
Mr. and Mrs. Leo Castelli, New York

Rebus, 1955 (fig. 10)
Combine painting, 8 feet x 12 feet
Mr. and Mrs. Victor Ganz, New York

Monogram, 1959 (fig. 9)
Construction, 48 x 72 x 72 inches
Moderna Museet, Stockholm

Trophy I (for Merce Cunningham), 1959 (fig. 8)
Combine painting, 66 x 41 inches
Galerie Beyeler, Basel, Switzerland

Empire II, 1961 (fig. 7)
Construction, 61 x 29 x 58 inches
Philip Johnson, New Canaan, Conn.

Reinhardt, Ad
(1913–67)

Number 119, 1958 (Black), 1958 (fig. 18)
Oil on canvas, 84 x 75 inches
The Hirshhorn Museum and Sculpture Garden,
    Smithsonian Institution, Washington, D.C.

Rivers, Larry
(b. 1923)

Study for George Washington Crossing the
    Delaware, 1953 (fig. 25)
Pencil, 11 x 13⅝ inches
The Museum of Modern Art, New York
Given anonymously

Study for George Washington Crossing the
    Delaware, 1953 (fig. 26)
Pencil, 11 x 13¾ inches
The Museum of Modern Art, New York
Given anonymously

Cézanne Stamp, 1963 (fig. 27)
Oil on canvas, 42 x 54 inches
The Hirshhorn Museum and Sculpture Garden,
    Smithsonian Institution, Washington, D.C.

Rosenquist, James
(b. 1933)

*F-111 (partial view), 1965 (pl. VIII)
Oil on canvas, with aluminum, entire work:
    10 feet x 86 feet
Mr. and Mrs. Robert C. Scull, New York

F-111, 1965 (fig. 29)
Oil on canvas, with aluminum, entire work:
    10 feet x 86 feet
Mr. and Mrs. Robert C. Scull, New York

Segal, George
(b. 1924)

The Butcher Shop, 1965 (fig. 23)
Plaster, wood, vinyl, metal and plexiglas,
    94 x 99¼ x 48 inches
Art Gallery of Ontario, Toronto
Gift from the Women's Committee Fund

Smith, Richard
(b. 1931)

Soft Pack, 1963 (fig. 16)
Oil on canvas, 8 feet 6 inches x 5 feet 8 inches
The Hirshhorn Museum and Sculpture Garden,
    Smithsonian Institution, Washington, D.C.

Stella, Joseph
(1877–1946)

Battle of Lights, Coney Island, 1913 (fig. 11)
Oil on canvas, 76 x 84 inches
Yale University Art Gallery, New Haven, Conn.

Stella, Frank
(b. 1936)

The Marriage of Reason and Squalor, 1959 (fig. 43)
Oil on canvas, 7 feet 6¾ inches x 11 feet ¾ inch
The Museum of Modern Art, New York
Larry Aldrich Foundation Fund

Still, Clyfford
(b. 1904)

1960-R (fig. 5)
Oil on canvas, 9 feet x 7 feet 3 inches
The Hirshhorn Museum and Sculpture Garden,
    Smithsonian Institution, Washington, D.C.

Torres-García, Joaquín
(1874–1949)

New York Street Scene, 1920 (fig. 3)
Oil on paper mounted on panel, 18½ x 26¼
    inches
The Hirshhorn Museum and Sculpture Garden,
    Smithsonian Institution, Washington, D.C.

Warhol, Andy
(b. 1930)

Green Coca-Cola Bottles, 1962 (fig. 30)
Oil on canvas, 82¼ x 57 inches
Whitney Museum of American Art, New York
Gift of the Friends of the Whitney Museum of
    American Art

*Numbers, 1962 (pl. XI)
Liquitex on canvas, 54 x 72 inches
Mr. and Mrs. Bagley Wright, Seattle

Electric Chair, 1966 (fig. 28)
Acrylic and silkscreen enamel on canvas,
    53¾ x 73¾ inches
Institute for the Arts, Rice University, Houston,
    Texas
De Menil Collection